This is a true story about
who lived over one hundr

1-99

Mary lived in Jamaica.
Her mother looked after sick people.
Mary wanted to help sick people too.
She wanted to be a nurse.

1

Soon Mary heard that a war had begun in
a country called Turkey.
She watched the soldiers leave Jamaica to
go and fight.
She wanted to go and help them.

2

Mary said, "I will ask the officers if I can
become a nurse."
The officers lived far away in London.
So Mary sailed to London to see them.

"We don't want your help," said the officers.
"Go away!"
But Mary did not give up.

She put on her blue bonnet with
red ribbons and sailed to Turkey.

There were soldiers who were hungry.
There were soldiers who were sick.
There were soldiers who were dying.

Mary built a kitchen and a place for
the soldiers to eat.

Every morning she got up at 4 o'clock to cook.
The cold and hungry soldiers smelled the
hot coffee and good food.
They came to Mary's kitchen for breakfast.

Then Mary put food and drink on the
back of her donkey.
She put a bag of medicine over her shoulder.
She walked to where the
soldiers were fighting.

"Get down!" the soldiers shouted.
"Go back! It is too dangerous!"
But Mary would not go back.

Every day the soldiers saw her walking
through the smoke.
They saw her blue bonnet with red ribbons.

She helped the soldiers who were
hungry, sick or dying.
Now she was a real nurse.

When the war ended Mary went
back to London.
Everyone had heard about Mary,
the brave and kind nurse.
People cheered her in the streets.

Mary wrote a book all about her life.
It was called "The Wonderful
Adventures of Mrs Seacole."

But when Mary grew old everyone
forgot about her.
When Mary died she was sad and alone.

In 1973 nurses came from Jamaica to put a special stone on Mary's grave.

HERE LIES
MARY
SEACOLE
1805~1881

OF KINGSTON JAMAICA
A NOTABLE NURSE WHO CARED
FOR THE SICK AND WOUNDED IN
THE WEST INDIES, PANAMA
AND ON THE BATTLEFIELDS
OF THE CRIMEA
1854~1856

So now we can remember Mary, the brave nurse with the blue bonnet and red ribbons.